RE...ES

cuf

by Janet Riehecky

Consultant: Jackie Gai, DVM
Wildlife Veterinarian

Raintree is an imprint of Capstone Global Library Limited, a company incorporated in England and Wales having its registered office at 264 Banbury Road, Oxford, OX2 7DY – Registered company number: 6695582

www.raintree.co.uk
myorders@raintree.co.uk

Edited by Kathryn Clay
Designed by Rick Korab and Juliette Peters
Picture research by Kelly Garvin
Production by Gene Bentdahl
Originated by Capstone Global Library LTD
Printed and bound in India.

ISBN 978 1 4747 3461 5 (hardback)
21 20 19 18 17
10 9 8 7 6 5 4 3 2 1

ISBN 978 1 4747 3469 1 (paperback)
22 21 20 19 18
10 9 8 7 6 5 4 3 2 1

British Library Cataloguing in Publication Data
A full catalogue record for this book is available from the British Library.

Acknowledgements
We would like to thank the following for permission to reproduce photographs: Alamy/John Cancalosi, 25 (top right); Minden Pictures: Mike Perry, 31 (bottom), Pete Oxford, 30 (tr), Stephen Dalton, 23 (middle); Newscom: Chris Mattison/FLPA/imageBROKER, 23 (tr), Mint Images/Frans Lanting, 22 (m); Science Source/Kenneth M. Highfill, 15 (b); Shutterstock: 108MotionBG, 6 (top left), A Jellema, 9 (b), ACEgan, 28-29, Alex Churilov, 1 (b), Anna Kucherova, 11 (tl), apiguide, 11 (top middle), Arto Hakola, 8 (b), Bill Frische, 18 (tr), BLFootage, 23 (tl), Camilo Torres, 19 (tm), Cathy Keifer, cover (bottom left), ChameleonsEye, 10 (right), choikh, 27 (top), Chokniti Khongchum, 22-23, cosma, 26 (left), Darkdiamond67, 24-25, Davdeka, 16-17, David Havel, back cover, 4 (r), E.O., 19 (tl), Fabien Monteil, 11, Firepac, 29 (t), foryouinf, 13 (b), Girish HC, 10, GUDKOV ANDREY, 31 (t), Heiko Kiera, 5 (t), 12-13, 13 (m), Honey Cloverz, 9 (m), hxdbzxy, 12 (b), Janelle Lugge, 16 (m), Jason Mintzer, 10 (ml), 11 (bm), Jason Patrick Ross, 17 (tl), JASON STEEL, 16 (t), jeep2499, 31 (m), jo Crebbin, 8-9, Joe McDonald, 25 (tl), komkrit Preechachanwate, 6-7, kosmos111, 14-15, Leena Robinson, 7 (b), Marek Velechovsky, 20-21, Matt Cornish, 25 (br), 26-27, Matt Jepson, cover (tl), 10 (t), 12 (t), 25 (bl), Michael Koenig, 6 (b), Mishkin_med, 2-3 (bkg), Mr. SUTTIPON YAKHAM, cover, (tr), Natalila Melnychuk, 22 (b), nattanan726, 1 (tr), Neil Burton, 22 (t), NickEvanKZN, 10 (mr), Nneirda, 19 (tr), Noppharat4569, 13 (t), Omaly Darcia, 32, Ondrej Prosicky, 18-19, Patrick K. Campbell, 30 (b), Philip Yb Studio, cover 1, (bkg), PorKaliver, 19 (b), Poul Riishede, 5 (b), reptiles4all, 7 (tr), 11 (bl), 14 (b), 15 (t), 24 (t), 28 (b), 30 (tl), Rich Carey, 17 (b), Robby Holmwood, 24 (b), Robert Eastman, 15 (m), Rudmer Zwerver, 11 (tr), Rusty Dodson, 11 (br), Sebastian Janicki, 1 (tl), Sergey Uryadnikov, 18 (tl), (m), SibFilm, 6 (tr), Signature Message, 17 (b), Skynavin, 10 (l), Songquan Deng, cover, (br), Sorbis, 4 (l), surassawadee, 28 (t), Stuart G Porter, 20 (b), Suede Chen, 7 (tl), Susan Schmitz, 4-5, Svoboda Pavel, 21, Teri Virbickis, 9 (tr), TongFotoman, 8 (t), Tony Campbell, 17 (tr), Utopia_88, 23 (b), Waclaw Bugno, 18 (b), YapAhock, 9 (tl), Yatra, 29 (b)

Artistic elements: Shutterstock: mishkin_med, nikiteev_konstantin, yyang, Z-art

CONTENTS

What are reptiles?

Reptiles are a group of animals that have dry, scaly skin or bony plates. Turtles, snakes and lizards are reptiles.

phylum
(FIE-lum)
a group of living things with a similar body plan; reptiles belong to the phylum Chordata (kawr-DEY-tuh); mammals, fish and amphibians are also in this group

kingdom
one of five very large groups into which all living things are placed; the two main kingdoms are plants and animals; reptiles belong to the animal kingdom

class
a smaller group of living things; reptiles are in the class Reptilia

order
a group of living things that is smaller than a class; there are four orders of reptiles

4

species
(SPEE-sees)
a group of animals that are alike and can produce young with each other; there are more than 10,000 species of reptiles

vertebrate
(VUR-tuh-brut)
an animal that has a backbone; reptiles are vertebrates

amphibian
(am-FI-bee-uhn)
a cold-blooded animal with a backbone, permeable skin and no scales; amphibians are not reptiles

cold-blooded
also called ectothermic (EK-tuh-THER-mik) cold-blooded animals have a body temperature that is the same as the air around them; reptiles are cold-blooded

5

scales
small, hard plates that cover a reptile's body

jaws
the bones of the upper and lower parts of the mouth; jaws hold teeth; saltwater crocodiles have the strongest jaws in the animal kingdom

beak
a sharp, pointy covering on the front of the jaw; turtles and tortoises have beaks

shell
a hard outer covering; shells keep turtles safe

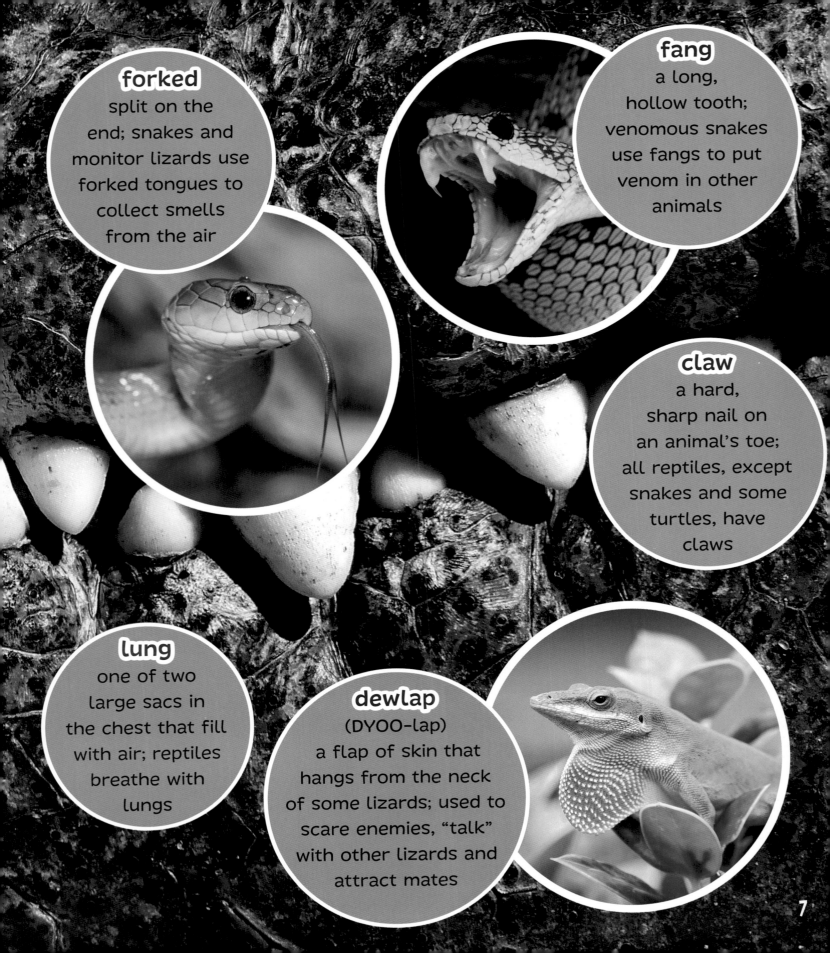

forked
split on the end; snakes and monitor lizards use forked tongues to collect smells from the air

fang
a long, hollow tooth; venomous snakes use fangs to put venom in other animals

claw
a hard, sharp nail on an animal's toe; all reptiles, except snakes and some turtles, have claws

lung
one of two large sacs in the chest that fill with air; reptiles breathe with lungs

dewlap
(DYOO-lap)
a flap of skin that hangs from the neck of some lizards; used to scare enemies, "talk" with other lizards and attract mates

Getting into groups

alligators
large, mostly freshwater reptiles with strong jaws and a rounded nose; the bottom teeth cannot be seen when the jaws are closed

crocodiles
look like alligators, but usually with a pointed nose; the bottom teeth can be seen when the jaws are closed; found in both freshwater and salt water

lizards
have four legs; most have dry, scaly skin

turtles

most have a hard shell into which they can pull their heads and legs; turtles have webbed feet and live mostly in water

tortoises

look like turtles but do not have webbed feet; tortoises live on land

tuataras

(too-uh-TAR-uhs) look like lizards, with two rows of teeth in the upper jaw that overlap a row of teeth in the lower jaw; found only in New Zealand

snakes

do not have legs; a snake's skin is covered in scales

Simply snakes

There are more than 3,000 species of snakes in the world. They come in all sizes, from small garter snakes to giant pythons.

garter snake
a mostly small, colourful snake commonly found North America; ga snakes may have yellow, green, blu or orange stripes

python
(PYE-thon): a large, non-venomo snake that kills by squeezing; py live mostly in Africa and Asia

cobra
(KOH-bruh): a large, venomous snake that spreads its neck skin to look like a hood

rattlesnake
a venomous snake with thick rings on its tail; rattlesnakes shake their tails as a warning to

mamba
a quick, venomous snake that can move faster than a person can run; the black mamba may be the world's deadliest snake

boa
(BOH-uh): a non-venom snake that squeezing; live in Cent South Ame female boa

Komodo dragon

(kuh-MOH-doh DRA-gun): the largest lizard in the world; Komodo dragons can grow up to 3 metres (10 feet) long and weigh up to 136 kilograms (300 pounds)

iguana

(ih-GWAH-nuh) a large, green tree-dwelling lizard with a spiny crest on its back

worm lizard

a legless lizard that looks like a snake

Lots of lizards

Think there are a lot of snake species? Lizards outnumber them! There are more than 4,600 species of lizards in the world.

chameleon

(kuh-ME-lee-on) a small, tree-dwelling lizard that can change its skin colour to match its surroundings

skink

the largest family of lizards; skinks have smooth, thick bodies and short limbs

gila monster

(HEE-luh mon-ster) a large, venomous lizard

gecko

(GEK-oh): a small, noisy lizard found in the tropics; unlike other lizards, geckos don't have eyelids, so they must lick their eyes clean

Circle of life

egg
most reptiles bury their eggs under ground; reptiles usually hatch in a few weeks, but Komodo dragons take seven to eight months

clutch
a group of eggs; reptile clutch sizes vary from 1 to more than 100 eggs

egg tooth
a sharp bump on top of the head; young reptiles use the egg tooth to break out of their shells

guard
to keep safe; most reptiles leave after laying their eggs, but some skinks, lizards, alligators and crocodiles guard their nests

nest

a structure built by animals to hold their eggs; the king cobra is the only snake that builds a nest for its eggs

hatchling

a young reptile that just came out of its shell; hatchlings look like small adults

live young

babies born directly from their mother, rather than from laid eggs; garter snakes have between five and 100 live young at one time

lifespan

the number of years a certain animal usually lives; the longest living reptiles are Galapagos tortoises (more than 100 years)

life cycle

the series of changes that take place in a living thing, from birth to death

natal beach

(NAY-tuhl BEECH): the place where a sea turtle hatches; sea turtles return to their natal beach to lay eggs of their own

Discovering the world

vibration
(vye-BRAY-shuhn)
a wave of movement;
instead of hearing
sounds, most reptiles
feel vibrations on
the ground

heat pit
a small hole on the
face of some snakes;
heat pits feel heat and
help snakes find food,
even in the dark

sight
chameleons
can move each
eye on its own;
they can look at two

Jacobson's organ
two small sacs on the roof of the mouth; snakes and lizards carry smells to the organ with their tongues; Komodo dragons can smell food up to 4 kilometres (2.5 miles) away

sensory pit
(SEN-suh-ree PIT): a small black speck on the jaws of alligators and crocodiles; sensory pits help animals find food underwater

touch
snakes feel their surroundings with their tongues

third eye
tuataras and some lizards have an "eye" on the tops of their heads that helps

Home, sweet home

Reptiles live on every continent, except Antarctica. They can be found both on land and in water.

meadow
a low-lying land covered with grass; grass snakes live in meadows

desert
(DEH–zuhrt)
a dry area that gets little rain; the thorny desert lizard and desert tortoise live in the desert

sea snake

ocean
a large body of salt water; about 100 types of reptiles live in oceans, including sea turtles, sea snakes and marine iguanas

swamp
a low-lying land often covered with water; snapping turtles and American alligators live in swamps

forest
a heavily treed area; box turtles, rattlesnakes and lizards live in forests

box turtle

snapping turtle

rainforest
a thick area of trees where rain falls almost every day; more than 450 types of reptiles live in the Amazon rainforest

freshwater
water that does not contain salt; various species of snakes, turtles and crocodiles live in freshwater rivers

crocodile

habitat
the type of place and conditions in which a plant or animal lives; reptiles live in many different habitats, including

Let's eat

A reptile's diet might include plants or animals. But reptiles eat much less than mammals and other warm-blooded animals. Why? Because their bodies don't have to make their own heat.

squeeze
boas and pythons squeeze prey to death before eating it

boa

Komodo dragons

scavenger
(SKAV-in-jer) an animal that feeds on animals that are already dead; Komodo dragons, monitors and most turtles are scavengers

bite
saltwater crocodiles stay underwater until prey is nearby, then lunge and bite with their huge jaws

carnivore
(KAHR-nuh-vor) an animal that eats only meat; alligators, crocodiles and snakes are carnivores

crush
to press very hard on something; African egg-eating snakes crush eggs in their mouths, swallow the food and spit out the shells

omnivore
(OM-nuh-vor): an animal that eats both plants and animals; bearded dragons are omnivores

tortoise

herbivore
(HUR-buh-vor): an animal that eats only plants; only a few reptiles, such as tortoises and the green iguana, are herbivores

swallow
some reptiles swallow food without chewing it; many snakes can open their mouths wide enough to swallow prey whole

Part of the chain

Reptiles are an important part of the food chain. They are both predators and prey.

energy
(EN-er-jee): the power needed to live; energy is passed through the food chain

ecosystem
(EE-koh-sis-tum): the connections between plants, animals and the earth that make up the living world

producer
(pruh-DO-ser): something that makes its own energy; plants are producers

consumer
(kuhn-SYOO-mer): an animal that needs to eat other things for energy; all reptiles are consumers

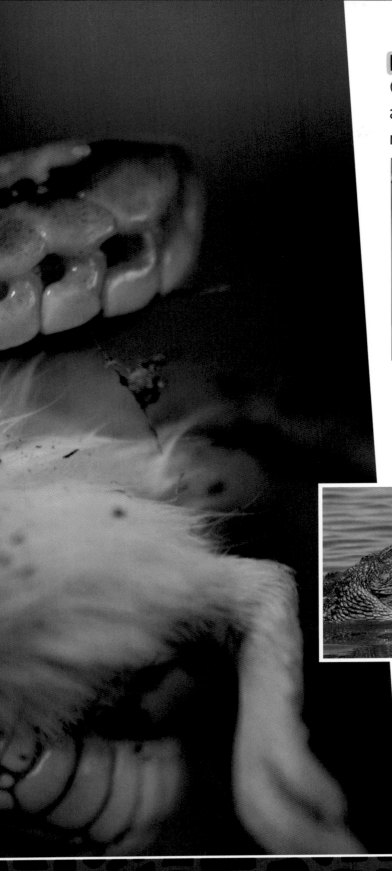

prey
(PRAY): an animal hunted by another animal for food; insects are prey for most reptiles

predator
(PRED-uh-tur): an animal that hunts other animals for food; most reptiles are predators

food chain
a series of living things in which each one eats the one before it; crocodiles are at the top of their food chain

plant seeds
when reptiles eat plants, the seeds come out in the reptile's waste; the seeds are buried into the soil, and new plants grow

Move it

Reptiles go from place to place in many different ways. Most move on four legs. Some run on two hind legs. Others don't move with legs at all!

dive
to plunge head first, usually into water; marine iguanas dive into the water to find plants to eat

glide
to move smoothly; Draco lizards glide between trees using flaps of skin like wings

burrow
to dig a hole or tunnel under ground; goanna lizards burrow under the ground to make dens

climb
most reptiles
can climb;
geckos have sticky
toes that grip
almost every
surface

tunnel
to dig
through the
ground; sandfish
skinks tunnel
through dry
sand

sprint
a short,
fast run; basilisk
lizards can sprint
across water on
their back legs

slither
to move
by twisting
and sliding;
rattlesnakes
slither

swim
many reptiles
can swim; crocodiles
use their large tails
to help them move
in the water

jump
most lizards
are good jumpers;
water dragons can
jump into the air to
catch a mosquito

Staying safe

Reptiles have many ways to stay safe. They may run away or hide. They may dig a hole in the sand or play dead – whatever it takes to keep from becoming lunch.

mimicry
(MIM-ih-kree)
the act of looking like something or someone else; some non-venomous reptiles look like venomous reptiles to trick predators to stay away

armour
hard, scaly skin that predators can't easily bite; when scared, armadillo girdled lizards roll into balls with their tails in their mouths

camouflage
(KA-muh-flahzh)
colouring that makes animals look like their surroundings; many snakes and lizards blend into the rocks, soil, leaves and tree bark where

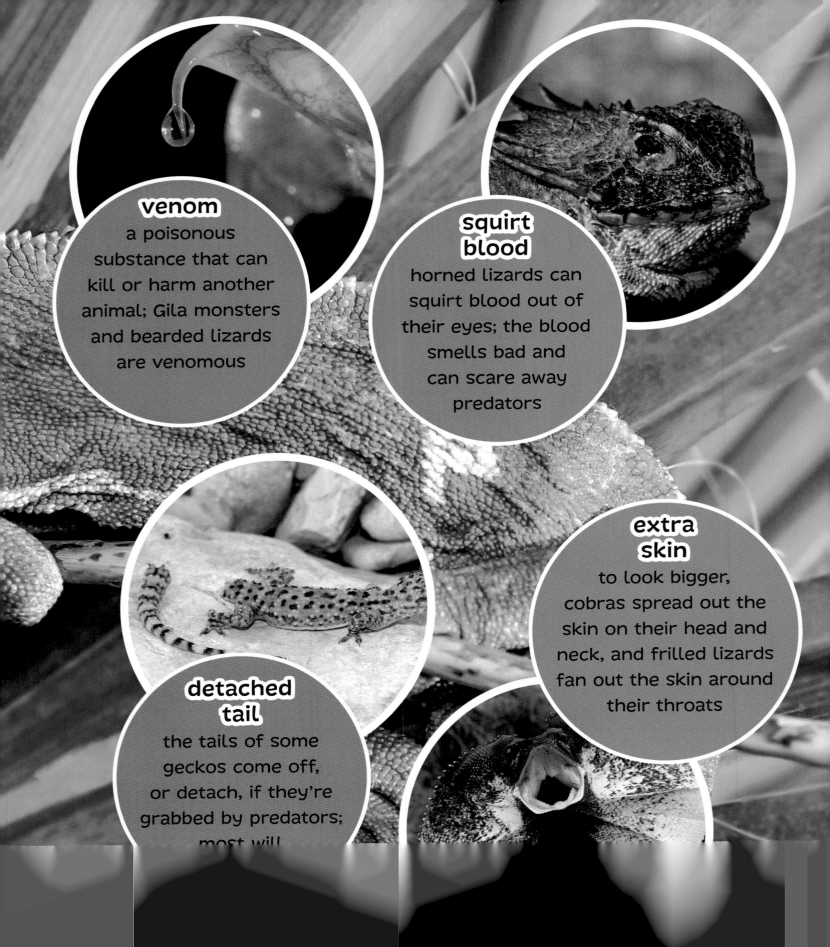

venom
a poisonous substance that can kill or harm another animal; Gila monsters and bearded lizards are venomous

squirt blood
horned lizards can squirt blood out of their eyes; the blood smells bad and can scare away predators

extra skin
to look bigger, cobras spread out the skin on their head and neck, and frilled lizards fan out the skin around their throats

detached tail
the tails of some geckos come off, or detach, if they're grabbed by predators; most will

Endangered!

Many reptiles are endangered. They are at risk of disappearing forever. Some are hunted. Others lose their homes or food sources when people build cities and roads.

extinct
(ek-STINGKT): no longer living; an extinct animal is one that has died out, with no more of its kind on Earth; dinosaurs are extinct reptiles

endangered
at risk of becoming extinct; Komodo dragons are endangered, numbering fewer than 6,000 in the wild

fossil
(FOSS-suhl): the remains or traces of living things preserved as rock; scientists found a lizard fossil that was 340 million years old

Chinese alligator
the rarest alligator in the world, numbering fewer than 150 in the wild

super croc
also called *Sarcosuchus*; an extinct reptile that lived 110 million years ago; it measured 12 metres (40 feet) long and weighed 9,000 kilograms (10 tons)

poacher
(POH-cher): a person who collects or kills animals illegally; in India more than 10,000 snakes are caught and sold by poachers each month

stegosaurus
a bony-plated dinosaur that fed on plants; stegosaurs had small heads and long, spiky tails

Tyrannosaurus rex
(ti-RAN-uh-sor-uhs REX): a huge carnivore that lived 68 to 66 million years ago; its closest living relatives are birds

Reptile records

oldest reptile
a radiated tortoise from Madagascar named Tu'I Malila lived to be nearly 190 years old

smallest reptile
the leaf chameleon of Madagascar measures only 25 millimetres (1 inch) long

longest flight
a flying gecko can glide up to 61 metres (200 feet) from tree to tree

fastest reptile on land
the spiny-tailed iguana can run up to 34 kilometres (21 miles) per hour

longest wait

tuatara young stay in their eggs for 12 to 15 months before they hatch

heaviest reptile

saltwater crocodiles can weigh between 400 and 1,000 kilograms (880 and 2,200 pounds)

fastest swimmer

a leatherback turtle can swim 35 kilometres (22 miles) per hour for short distances

longest reptile

a python found in Indonesia in 1912 measured more than 9.8 metres (32 feet) long

Fun facts

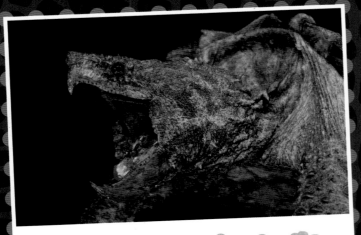

An **alligator snapping turtle** tricks its prey. Most of its body is buried in mud. A small piece of red skin dangles from its mouth. Fish think the skin is a worm and try to eat it. Instead they get snapped up.

When a **box turtle** tucks its head into its shell, a piece of shell covers the opening.

Anacondas can live for months without eating.

When in danger, **Komodo dragons** vomit to decrease their weight. They are able to run faster with an empty stomach.

In 1999, a scientist at the San Diego Zoo discovered that **monitor lizards** could count the snails they were given for dinner. They could count up to six.

The **giant leatherback turtle** is one of the few reptiles that is warm-blooded. It produces heat in its body by squeezing a muscle.

FIND OUT MORE

Remarkable Reptiles (Extreme Animals), Isabel Thomas (Raintree, 2012)

Reptiles (Eyewonder) (DK, 2013)

Snakes and Lizards (Really Weird Animals), Clare Hibbert (Franklin Watts, 2012)

Why Do Reptiles Have Scales? (Wildlife Wonders), Pat Jacobs (Franklin Watts, 2014)

WEBSITES

animals.nationalgeographic.com/animals/reptiles
Visit this National Geographic website to find lots of information about reptiles.

www.arkive.org/reptiles
This website has videos and information about some amazing reptiles.

Vivienne knew what she had to do.

It wasn't going to be easy, **but it had to be done.**

"Stand back, everyone!" she yelled.

Vivienne knew what she had to do.

It wasn't going to be easy, **but it had to be done.**

"Stand back, everyone!" she yelled.